365 Morning Messages

from the Angels

Daily Messages to Guide You to

a More Positive Life

Carol.
The angels love you
♡
Elana

Received by Elana Whyte

Wings by Howard Koverman

Cover photography by Phyllis Hunt

ISBN: 978-0-9979338-0-2

Guided Awareness Publishing

Dedication

This book is dedicated to everyone

who has angels around them.

This means you.

Thank you Angels for sharing these beautiful
messages with me so I may share
them with the world.

Thank you to my family who have supported my
journey so far with such love and laughter.

Thank you to everyone who requested the morning
angel message texts. I feel so blessed to have been
able to share them with you.

And thank you to those who encouraged me to
compile them in this book.

Namaste

HOW THIS BOOK CAME ABOUT

Beginning another school year as a school psychologist in an inner city, I was apprehensive about how the year would be. Each year has seemed to be more challenging and I hoped this year would be different. The night before school began, a thought popped into my head, "We need a daily pick-me-up!" I had an urge to share a positive message with my friends to help us stay strong each day. What kind of message? I had no idea. I just felt strongly that I needed to offer them. So I texted a few close school friends and asked if they would like to receive a positive text message before school the next morning. They accepted and I went to bed not sure of what I had just offered. I figured I would open one of my inspirational books, pull something out, and send it off.

Well, that obviously was not the plan, for the next morning came and I was inspired to sit quietly and "get" a message. I thought, "Why not?" The worst thing that could happen is I pull out an inspirational book. So I sat on the edge of my bed, lights out, palms up open to the universe, and closed my eyes. "All is well! Believe!" popped into my head. Okay! That's a great message. I'll send it.

The following morning I did the same thing, but this time I saw a mountain and then the view from it. I thought a bit and the message that formed was "As we climb the mountain, it is the views that we have to remember." Each morning I would get pictures and/or words and a message was formed. So exciting! What was even more exciting was that my friends began talking to others and more and more people asked if I would send the messages to them. I received a message almost daily until there were 365 of them, one for every day of the year. By the time I stopped, I was sending them to over 60 people just by word of mouth. Amazing!

When I decided to stop sending them out, many asked if I was going to compile them in a book. A book? Why not! So these are the messages. I hope they are as inspiring, uplifting, and thought provoking as they were for me and my friends.

Sending love and light to you on your journey with the Angels.

HOW TO USE THIS BOOK

The messages are in the order received
beginning the last week of August (the first
week of school in Connecticut). So you can go
in calendar order, if you prefer.

Or start on the first day you pick up the book
and go in order each day.

And/or pick up the book whenever you are
guided, open up to a page,
and read the message.

There is no wrong way to use this book.
However you are guided, go for it!

All is well!
Believe!

As we climb the
mountain, it is the
view we need
to remember.

As we navigate
the potholes
in the road,
we need to always
be aware of the
light ahead of us.

Just like a
lighthouse keeper,
shine your light
for all to see.

Every person is a
flower blooming
and growing at
their own pace.

Everything is as it
should be for our
ultimate growth

Be playful and
laugh as often
as possible.

We can soar with
the right attitude.

Just like when you
travel, pack only
what you need and
leave the rest behind.

The fuel we
supply our mind,
body, and spirit will
determine how we
sail through life.

The view from a
hot air balloon
may be daunting,
but there is no other
experience like it.
Take chances.
Enjoy life.

Be aware of your
surroundings,
but not so much
that you lose your
inner being.

Share your experiences with like-minded people to truly enjoy life.

Seeing something
through another's
view is experiencing
something you
have never
experienced before.

Life is like
painting a picture.
Sometimes we
don't like the strokes,
but we should
continue to strive for
a masterpiece.

Don't let your
ego dominate your
worth. You are
capable of
amazing things.

Trust your inner guidance to see through the dark smoke surrounding some people.

Trust and believe!
Your thoughts
are powerful.
Make them
good ones.

Letting go and allowing the universe to show you real truth will bring you more joy and fulfillment than you could ever imagine.

There are
mysteries of the
world that we do
not yet understand,
but we can
understand what
happens in our own
lives if we remember
there is a reason
and purpose for
everything.

Be grateful for
even the little
annoyances, for
without them you
may not recognize all
the good in your life.

If you ever feel alone, remember there is a whole world of people and many adventures to explore. Allow the universe to guide you to the right ones for you.

Just because
things aren't
proven, doesn't
mean they don't exist.
Believe in the
possibilities!

Trusting the universe's bird's eye view of the full picture will allow us to navigate over the rolling hills ahead of us.

Breathing in
the smoke of the
city may or may
not make you sick.
Breathing in the
negativity surely will.
Counteract that
negativity by sending
out love to the
environment
surrounding you.

Through remembering challenging past experiences, you can have the strength to know that you will also survive and grow through current and future ones.

Do not allow
reruns of old
experiences to
clutter your mind.
Be in the here and
now to fully enjoy
new experiences
because right now,
in this moment,
all is well.

When wrestling
with a dilemma,
go with your heart.

Allow your emotions to flow naturally. Speeding through them will only allow you to feel the bumpy waves like riding a speedboat.

Even though
things may not
go as you planned,
trust that that is
part of the plan.

You have to ask
the universe for
it to be given. First,
let go of what you
don't want, then be
open to receive what
you have asked for.

When you are
deep in a forest,
hold onto the light
that shows through
the trees.

Meditate
a little every day.
It will change
your life.

Remember to
stop for a moment
to look up at the
sky and breathe in
the beauty of what
nature brings us.

Don't run
because of fear.
Feel it and let it go,
as everything is in
divine order and
you are safe.

Just as a driver
of a dump truck
is in control of
what, where, and
why he dumps his
stuff, you are in
control of dumping
your stuff. Give it to
the earth to recycle
into positive energy.

Open to the
offerings of the
universe.
You are protected.

Pay attention to
the sounds around
you, as they can be
messages.

Don't assume what another says is bull until you look through their eyes to see their perspective. We all have our own telescope to bring things closer to view.

We are entitled
to our piece of the
pie. Keep your
flame of desire
burning to draw
it in and allow
it to manifest.

Find your inner
sanctuary when
things feel
uncomfortable.

Through the unstable feelings, as when on a rocking boat in a bad storm, remember the sun always eventually shines through.

You know what
you need to do!
Listen to your
inner guidance.
It will never steer
you wrong.

Our personal
history makes us
who we are.
Embrace it.

Looking
through dark
glasses will not
give you a clear
understanding.
Looking through
joyous visualizations
will help brighten
your path.

Go outside
and allow the
sun to burn away
all negative feelings
and wrap yourself
in the air of
unconditional love.

Love is the
most powerful
thing in the
universe. Sending
it out to everything
in your life will bring
the same back to you.

When you feel
that things aren't
going your way, do
not give up your
power or energy to
others, but rather
take an aerial view
of your life and
be grateful for
what you see.

Be honest
with yourself.
Dig deep for those
messages that you
repeat to yourself.
Are they healthy?

Try to find a few
minutes today to
just sit and be.

Ahead of us,
the future is vast.
Behind us, the
past should be
small. Stay in this
moment where
it is clear.

Be not afraid
of what you
don't know. You
have the power to
manifest your
desired outcomes.
It's your journey.

On the surface
things may be
out of balance,
but you have the
power to go deep
and release.

Sometimes we
need to float
downstream and
not fight the current.

The light inside
you is bright and
can overcome
any obstacle.

Affirm what you
want your future
to look like and
make it happen.

Be patient
with yourself.

Honor your
primal feelings.
Keep the ones that
bring you peace.

Let go of the
thoughts that
bind you and
travel in your mind
to wherever you want
your life to go.

Painting
images of your
desires can flow
as freely as water
falling freely over a
waterfall. Let go and
enjoy the process.

Allow things to
flow naturally
as in nature.
Everything in nature
has a purpose. We
do not have to know
them all to listen,
see, and feel the
magnificence.

Each day look
yourself in the
eye and say,
"I love you."
If it's difficult,
keep practicing.

Life can feel like
a runaway train.
Simplifying can
bring peace.

We all are
distracted by
our thoughts.
If they do not serve
you, release them.
Ask the angels
for assistance,
if needed.

The ladder of success is not measured by how much money we bring in. It is about how much love we send out.

Signs can be seen
out every window
that will help guide
you to a carefree life.

When you are
finding life rocky
and even a little
scary, focus on the
smaller positive
interactions with
others that feel good.

Imagine
obsessive worries
floating on a far
away ship over
the horizon.
Then breathe.

Try not to make things more than they are. Allow your higher self to guide you and feel it in your heart.

Listening to
uplifting positive
music will help
surround yourself
with positive energy.

Compliments
are treasures we
should keep in a
treasure chest in
our hearts. Try to
keep the chest full
by accepting them
rather than negating
them with self-talk.

We have
choices. We can
complain and
draw more misery
with our thoughts
or we can feel good
about who we are in
every moment and let
those thoughts guide
us to better times.

Things are not always what they seem. Share to learn and understand the possibilities.

Just as a blimp
looks smaller in
the sky than it
truly is, imagine
worries becoming
smaller as you move
them further away.
Then fill the
larger space with
healing light.

When you have
large walls up,
start by opening a
drawbridge to allow
some sweetness
through that
awaits you.

Sometimes our
destinations seem
unclear as we row
down the stream
of life, but we
eventually reach the
shore, which takes
us to our next
destination.
Keep the light with
you on your journey.

As we nurture
our mind and
spirit with these
morning messages,
remember that the
body is part of the
mind, body, spirit
alignment. Try to make
choices that nurture
your body as much as
possible.

When things aren't going as you plan, stop, go within, and know that everything is okay.

Pay attention
to the beauty
around you like
your family, flowers,
or a hawk soaring
across the sky. They
will lift your heart.

Be proud of
who you are and
what you have
accomplished.

Worrying
about what may
happen in the
future only
interferes with the
beauty of our now.
Be in this moment...
and this moment...
and this moment...

When something
unexpected
happens in your
life that knocks
you off balance,
remember it is part
of the journey.

The more we
know, the more
we understand.
There are many
authors writing
about spiritual topics.
Ask and you will be
guided to ones that
resonate with you.

Open the lids
to your
compartmentalized
emotions and allow
them to flow.
Feel them,
understand them,
and keep the ones
that feel good.

Carefully observe dogs with their owners. You will learn a great deal about true unconditional love.

Think like an innocent young child. Feel the lightheartedness and smile at everyone.

Nurturing yourself includes taking a break from a fast-paced day. For example, instead of cooking the planned meal, stop and get some nutritious takeout and relax.

Getting through
challenging
situations can give
us a feeling of
freedom.
Celebrate them.

Even when
struggling,
love yourself.
You are doing the
best you can.

When you feel
like you are
jumping through
hoops, be grateful
you have hoops.

Hold onto the feeling of being blessed while working through life. Life won't feel so much like work.

Being mindful
in the present
moment will help
keep you balanced
in the light.

Being grateful
for ALL
experiences
helps our soul
learn and grow while
staying in the light.

When you are
having difficulty
concentrating
or you are
overwhelmed,
go outside. Feel the
earth beneath your
feet and breathe in the
outside air, no matter
how cold it is.

Embrace the
surprises around
every corner.

Forgive,
for the negative
emotions only hurt
ourselves. Have the
courage to let go of
the hurt and replace
it with self-love.

Some of our
reactions are
responses to the
energetic input all
around us.
Remember to breathe.

If the ancient people could build the Great Wall of China and the Pyramids, then we know we are capable of doing what we think is impossible.

Change your
thinking and
change the world!

When you are
feeling frustrated,
upset, or things
"aren't going right,"
stop, breathe, and
focus on the blessings
around the situation
and watch how
things change.

You can protect
yourself by staying
calm and being in
the higher vibration
of love.

Imagine
beautiful white
light flowing
through and
around you to
bring you peace.

Keep the "bull"
at a distance
and your road
will be clear.

Just as trees
bend to weather
storms, we can
bend to weather
challenging situations.

Ask to be
guided to the
people and places
you need to achieve
your desires.
Then be open to
recognizing them.

Just as we shift
our position
when someone or
something obscures
our view of a
beautiful sunset,
we may need to
shift to see the
beauty in life.

Sometimes
just being in
the silence is the
best time spent.

Take time to put
the unnecessary
stuff for a nap and
allow your inner
child out to play.

The wolf and deer live in harmony until the wolf gets hungry. Then he only takes what he needs and leaves the rest for others. Live well, but in harmony.

Worrying is
like trying to
drive an old car
up a snowy hill.
You will be sliding
back and getting
stuck. Releasing the
worry and holding the
intention of a smooth
ride will allow you to
avoid the hill.

Do things that
bring you joy,
no matter how
small. This will
bring joy into your
life, which will draw
more joy to you.

Building a
fortress of love
from your heart
will protect you
from the crashing
waves of others and
help keep you
grounded.

Find the music
that lightens your
heart and makes
you dance.
Listen to it often!

Riding the
wave without
always seeing
what is in front of
us is faith. Trust
that everything is
in divine order and
enjoy the ride.

Awareness
brings growth.
Through growth,
things will change.
Allow your inner
guidance to guide
you through
the transitions.

Feel the
exhilaration
of taking risks.
Fear is boring
and stagnant.

Breath gives us
life. It can be
restricted and
hold us back or it
can be freeing. Pay
attention to your
breath in different
situations. See how it
changes with your
awareness.

During our transformation through our growth, we are attempting to maintain balance. Living in harmony with the earth and others is balance. Be kind to yourself on the journey.

Celebrate and
enjoy the rain as
it gives life to all
living things.

Finding peace
in the world will
only happen when
we find peace within
ourselves. Forgiveness
helps lead to that
peace and is for
ourselves, not the
other person.

Remember to
be in the present
so as to not miss
out on the magical
moments of the day.

There is enough
time to do all you
want to do if you
believe there is.

Approaching
everything with
love, even things
that are frustrating,
will nurture a more
positive life overall.

Things may
not be clear to
others from the
outside, but you
know your deep
inner strength and
connectedness
through love. Cut
the cords connected
to negativity.

You may be
afraid for a cat
sitting high in an
open window, but
from his perspective,
there is a beautiful
view that you cannot
appreciate from below.

Do everything
with love and
observe how your
life changes.

Although you
may not always
know where you
are going, trust it
is where you are
supposed to be.

Your memories of the past year may be happy and/or sad. Remember they are in the past. What you think about now becomes your future so enjoy your now. Use your manifesting power to make this year an awesome one!

Worry just gets
in the way of your
faith that your life
is in divine order.
Trust that it is as
it should be.

When you feel
all tied up like a
perfect bow, cut
your way out and
allow your emotions
to flow, as our
emotions are our
guidance system.

Radiate your
light and you will
always have warmth
around you.

Exercise,
meditation,
relaxation...
How do we fit
them all in?
Tell ourselves we can
and then believe!

When you
keep driving the
same road and
arriving at the
same undesirable
destination, look
around to change
your perspective to
see other avenues.

Although some
may not
understand,
we need to follow
our inner guidance,
much like animals
follow their instincts,
to find harmony.

Although the meanings of dreams are often not obvious, they are guidance from our soul. Pay attention to them.

Look for the
blessings in every
challenge of life.
You are powerful,
even during those
challenges as you
bring great blessings
to you by shielding
yourself from
the negativity.
Ask the angels
to help you.

Allow yourself
to be supported
by others instead
of containing
"problems," which
can be immobilizing.
Attract people who
can help you through
the healing process.

Rather than hiding from or warding off lower energy individuals, radiate love wherever you go. This will open a path for you to walk through.

If you show the
world the real
and true you,
you will draw
others like you to
you where you will
feel even more
comfortable to be you.

As you learn
to sit quietly in
the silence away
from distractions
a little each day, you
will become more
aware of the guidance
offered to you. You will
also feel better.

You are brave!

Learn from the
turtle. Taking
time to observe
your surroundings
will allow you to see
the beauty.

Believe, believe,
believe...
in yourself.

Surround
yourself with
little things that
are visual reminders
of the beauty in your
life. Then pay
attention to them.

Opening to the
guidance is the
first step to hearing
it. Let everything else
go and listen.

When your
mind is cluttered,
it is difficult to see
your path. Clear
your mind by
remaining in the
present moment
and enjoy the view.

Everyone is on their own path and doing the best they can. If you become upset with someone, look inward to see what triggered you.

Fear only
blocks our inner
knowing. Use your
breath to clear any
anxiety and allow
your guidance
to be heard.

Remember to
act out of love
and watch the
beauty in your life
unfold. This includes
love for yourself.

Everyone is on
their own path,
finding their own
way in their own way.
Being compassionate
towards others will
smooth your path.

Living in the
past only brings
heartache. Holding
onto poor memories
only prolongs
suffering. Longing to
relive good memories
hinders growth.
Cherishing today will
bring many good
things in the future.

When you experience a wonderful feeling, pay close attention to it, hold onto it as long as you can, and go back to it as often as possible. This will manifest more of the same in your future.

Gratefulness
is the key to
happiness. Generate
a list of anything
and everything you
are grateful for, no
matter how small you
may think something
is. As your list grows,
watch your life
transform.

Pay close
attention to your
intuition this week.
Separate it from any
anxiety. Trust it.
See where it takes you.

If we only
want people in
our lives that make
us feel good, then
we need to stop and
think about how we
talk to others if we
want to be someone
they want in theirs.

Just because
we cannot see
something with
our own eyes,
does not mean it
does not exist.
Be open to what
others see.

Sayings such as "Follow your dreams" may sound like old clichés, but read them again with a spiritual eye and new inspiration will follow.

Sometimes we
feel like we are
fighting upstream,
but like the salmon,
there is purpose.

As human
beings, we say
we are not perfect,
but we are. We
are perfect in this
moment on our path
because everything is
as it should be for us
to have the experiences
we are supposed to
have for our growth.

Go within to find
all the answers you
are looking for.

We can find
something to be
grateful for in every
experience, even a
noise from outside.
Take the time to find
what it is.

Being in the
present moment
is very powerful,
even if in that
moment you
are planning.

When things
are not going as
you would like, ask
yourself why. Our
lives are directly
related to how we
take care of ourselves
mentally, emotionally
and physically.
Remember, everything
has a purpose.

When we
are feeling
overwhelmed,
we need to retreat,
go within, and just
be with ourselves for
a little while. Then
things will be clearer.

Sometimes
when we stick
our necks out to
take chances, it
does not go as we
plan, but this is part
of our larger plan to
gain from our
experiences.

Pay attention
to the difference
in how your body
feels when you have
a negative thought
and a positive one.
This is what you are
sending out, which in
turn comes back to
you. Which do
you prefer?

Just like when
you are driving
around a large
bend in the road
and you cannot see
what is ahead, you
must trust that you
are safe when you do
not know what is
ahead in life. Let go of
the past fears and
enjoy the course
you are on.

Thinking the
world was flat
meant that there
was an end.
Knowing the world
is round means
endless possibilities.

Changing envy
into joy for the
other person will
bring more of what
you yearn for into
your life.

Know that deep
inside you know
the answers. Take a
"leap of faith"
when it is calling you.

Risky behaviors that can result in harm to ourselves, may provide a good feeling for a brief time, but they do not bring us true joy. True joy comes from pursuing what fulfills us from within.

As we strive to joyfully live in the moment, we need to make choices that will prepare us for a long and healthy life.

Our moods are
not contingent
on what others do
to us. It is a result
of our reaction. Look
deep within and be
open to learning why
you react the way you
do, how to release
what is unwanted, and
how to grow from the
experiences.

Rejuvenate
your soul.
Allow yourself to
fully be in the quiet.

When you are
feeling unbalanced,
look to the angels,
God, the universe...
for guidance to
feel better.

Sometimes we have feelings we are not proud of. Feel them, forgive yourself, and let them go. This is part of the human experience.

If we truly
put ourselves in
other's "shoes" and
really think about
why they do what
they do, we will
begin to have more
compassion for others.
We all have history
that makes us
who we are.

When you
find yourself with
worried or obsessed
thoughts, close your
eyes, imagine golden
light around your
head, and release the
thoughts to the
universe. Then forgive
yourself. Everything is
in divine order.

Miracles can
happen when we
remember to feel
the joy in our lives
and ask and are
open to help from
God, the angels,
the universe...

Continue to
ask for what you
want and believe
that the most
difficult times
are in the past.
Focus on the various
ways prosperity is
manifesting in your
life right now.

Although there may
be waves, there is
always light.

Find a
technique to
release worrying
thoughts, such
as placing an image
in a bubble and
watching it slowly
float away up into the
sky. Pay attention to
the feeling of release
and calm as it gets
smaller. Repeat as
often as needed.

Embrace the
past as it holds
everything that
made you you, but
do not live there.

Believe in
yourself for you
are the only one
who truly knows
what brings you joy.

Pay attention to your breath as it will guide you to understanding how you are handling all situations.

When
contemplating a
decision, trust your
inner feeling/
knowing, pushing
aside any anxiety/fear
of the outcome.

Our time is to be
shared with people
who help us feel good.

Support comes
in a variety of
ways. Let go of
expectations and
embrace whatever
type of support
another can give while
on their own journey.

Putting your
whole heart
and soul into
everything you do
in each moment will
bring you more of
what your heart
and soul loves.

If you are
feeling in any
way that does not
feel good to you,
take some deep
breaths of fresh air
and release.

When thinking about others, instead of making judgments about their past, see how their past has helped them grow into the person you know today. Decide if the person today is healthy for your life.

Follow your
inner knowing
and let go of what
does not serve you.
Only you know what
is right for you.

When feeling worried or down, open to the gifts of God, the universe, the angels... They are always sending you love, guidance, and protection to help you let go. Trust they are there.

Being who we
are can be
challenging at
times, but being
true to ourselves is
most important.
Look deep within to
find what truly feels
right for you and
follow it.

Regret just
brings our
energy down. It
is all about the
experience and
what we learn from it.
Forgive yourself
and move on.

We only get a
peek into how
someone else is
feeling because we
have not experienced
exactly what they have
throughout their life.
Being compassionate
not only helps heal
them, but heals
our own hearts.

Be kind to
yourself when
things are not going
as you would like.

Our souls are
intertwined with
every person we
meet on some level
for a purpose. Part
of our growth is to
accept that purpose.

Life is like bowling. The ball will go where your true focus and concentration is. So will your life.

Wonderful
things sometimes
come from the
most unexpected
encounters. Be open
as you never know
where they will lead.

As we walk through the forest, we must trust that there is a clearing ahead as we enjoy the beauty of the nature around us.

As you ask
God, the angels,
the universe...for
things that will
enhance your life,
be open to receiving
them as they may
not come in the
form you expect.

Many paths
have challenges.
We can choose to
call them obstacles
or experiences. Pay
attention to how
you feel with each
label and where
they could take you.

Before getting
out of bed in the
morning, affirm it
is a good day.
Imagine and feel
what that would
look like. Continue
throughout the day
and pay attention to
how your day goes.

Pick an "I am..." statement you can say to yourself throughout the day such as I am strong, I am productive, I am loved. As you say it, feel it. Assess how you did at the end of the day.

As you really
pay attention to
the taste of your
food, your body
will crave healthier
choices. We know
deep inside what we
need to do. Honor
yourself and do it.

The mind, body, spirit connection is powerful. Taking care of yourself emotionally is just as important as taking care of your physical body as illness stems from how we are dealing with life emotionally.

Love is
everywhere.
Begin to recognize
even the smallest
acts of kindness,
which is love, and you
will begin to notice
more love come
into your life.

The smallest
gesture toward
someone can
change their day
and yours.
Make it positive.

Our interactions
with others are
very important.
Our messages to
others are very
important. Be kind
in the delivery as
everyone is doing the
best they can with
what they know.

People may
not react to
your kindness as
you expect. Let go
of your expectations
and allow them to be
who they are in that
moment. That is all
they can be.

Animals are
here to help us
learn unconditional
love and compassion.
Remember to give
yours as much love
and attention as
possible. It is a win-
win situation.

Try to look at
everything with
love today and see
how different you
feel tonight.

Believe in yourself.
You have everything
you need within you.

If something
feels like a hassle,
then we must
change our thinking
about it. What we
think, is.

When feeling
overwhelmed,
look at what you
have accomplished
and then in the
moment, decide
your next step.

Our body is
the protector of
our soul and thus
is as beautiful as
our soul. Stand
naked in front of
the mirror and love
what you see, as you
are a beautiful human
being inside and out.

Life is like a
Ferris wheel.
Respect diversity
as some may like
the ride and some
may not. Also, take
it slow and enjoy
the view that is not
usually in your
line of vision.

In this
stimulating
world, try to take
time to go back to
the simple things.
Get outside, connect
with animals, and
enjoy the simplicity
of it all.

Tap into the power
of love to let go
of fears.

The mind/body connection is more powerful than we can imagine. Dealing on a deep level with our true inner feelings and thoughts does positively impact our bodies.

Taking risks
is part of the
growth process.
Ask yourself what
would be the worst
that could happen.
Ask the same question
again to your response
and continue this
process until you are
comfortable. Then
enjoy the experience.

We are all
intuitive. Pay
attention to your
deep inner knowing
and let it guide you.
You have all the
answers you need
within you.

A whole
new world
is developing.
Seeing and doing
things through love
will help the shift as
it helps each of us
individually.

How our
bodies feel is
directly connected
to the foods we
eat. Refrain from
processed foods and
drink only water for
a few days. Pay
attention to how
your body feels.

Even if you
do not love
something you
are doing, send the
situation love. It will
raise your vibration
so you feel better
about it.

Supporting
each other is part
of our life purpose.
Open your heart to
spread love to others
and allow others to
support you. Your life
will flourish in
response.

There is no
sinning, only
learning. Forgive
yourself and others
to grow and be
truly happy.

Our emotions
help us feel our
inner knowing.
Allow them to flow
as they guide us to
make the best
choices for ourselves.

Life is hard
only if you fight
it. Let go and follow
what you know is
right deep down
for you.

Be grateful
when someone
asks you for help.
It means you have
the faculties to do so.

With any
dis-ease, our
attitude about
it is extremely
important. Our
minds are a
key part of the
recovery process.

Resisting change results in disharmony. Allow the natural changes of life to occur for a smoother transition.

Other's actions only
impact us in how
we respond.

You can experience through watching others or by doing it yourself. Either is fine as long as it is what you truly want to do.

Everyone has
a right to their
own feelings. We
do not have to
understand or
agree with them
to respect that
they have them.

Open your
heart when
meeting people of
cultures different
from your own.
There is much to
be learned through
those experiences.

Notice the
beauty in nature
around you such as
the sky and grass...
It will help ground
you to be in the
moment and bring
joy to your day.

Life may feel
like it is going
fast, but instead of
complaining about
or fearing the speed,
enjoy the ride.

Try not to hide
from experiences
because of fear.
Experiencing the
falls helps us learn
how not to fall.

Sometimes we must go through things that do not feel good. They are part of the life process. Trust the process. You are safe.

The ocean represents our emotions such as calmness, excitement, and anger. Think about how you ride through the changes because the ocean is never stagnant.

Feel the wind
in your hair,
feel the sun on
your face, pay
attention to the
beauty around you.

Resistance to
what is only
results in
frustration and
disappointment.
Breathe and
find your path
without resisting.

Looking for
positive change?
Look in the mirror
daily and say,
"I love you!"
until you believe it.

Life is like a
hike in the
woods. You could
walk through the
river or walk over
the bridge. Which
path would you take
to reach your
destination with the
least amount of stress
and struggle?

Always
searching for
something better
does not allow us
to appreciate what
we have. There is
positive in everything.
We just have to
recognize it.

By not fully accepting compliments, you reduce your vibration and self-love. Embrace all compliments. You are deserving of them.

No one can
"make us mad."
When we become
angry, something
within us has been
triggered. We choose
how to react to all
situations.

There is beauty
under the surface.
Allow it to show.

When your
mind is racing
with thoughts,
focus on your
breath as you take
a few deep breaths.
With practice, your
mind will clear so you
are better able
to focus.

Free your
spirit by following
your life purpose.
Not sure what that
is? Try things out
until you find what
fills you with joy.

We are beings
of extensive
possibilities.
Release the fear
that is holding
you back.

Music is powerful.
It can help change
your mood.
Choose it wisely.

Make a list of positive "I am" statements. Believe them when you say them daily. Pay attention to how you feel and how things change.

Doing the
right thing
may be hard,
but think about
how much growth
you will have from
the experience.
It will also make
your soul soar.

Some people
are like cactus.
They have spines
(spikes) to protect
themselves. Show
compassion and
understanding for
your well-being
and theirs.

Put the intention of love into everything you give, material or not. It will be better received and reciprocated.

There is always a
few minutes to be
kind to others.

Sharing in the joy of others makes us feel good. Surround yourself with people who share their joys more than their woes.

Although the
ride maybe rough,
have faith that it
will smooth out and
that all is well.

Sometimes things need to be said to help with growth. Be mindful of the delivery.

Our lives are
like approaching
a yellow traffic
light. We can stop,
slow down, or go for
it. All are okay as
long as we choose
our true soul's desire.

Try not to be
hurt or offended
if someone does
not accept your
kindness. They are
in their own place
and it is not an
indication of
your worth.

Just love.

Society may not
understand what
our hearts want,
but we need to
follow it anyway.

Be proud of your
accomplishments
no matter the size.
Let them overshadow
anything that might
bring you down.

Pay attention
to the signs that
lead you to
opportunities being
aligned just for you.
Our resistance is the
only thing holding
us back.

If something
does not go the
way you planned,
it was how it was to
be. In hindsight you
will understand, if
you allow yourself
to see.

Outer space is
limitless.
So are we.
Imagine it.
Feel it.
Believe it.

Worrying
about what you
think will happen
not only wastes
time, but manifests
exactly what you do
not want. Stay positive
in the now.

Pay attention
to your
surroundings.
It will help keep
you in the present
moment where you
always want to be.

When we do
not get something
we want, there is
good reason. Trust
that everything is as
it should be for us to
experience what we
need to on our
journey.

Think about
the connection
you have with
others. Are you
enhancing their life
in a positive way?

Multi-tasking
is good for
some situations;
however, your
attention is limited.
Focusing on one
thing helps keep
you in the present
moment, which
enhances your
life overall.

Pay attention to your body. It is giving you signs of what it needs physically, emotionally, and spiritually.

Forgive yourself
through the
struggle and it
will not be such
a struggle.

Stepping out
of our comfort
zone can lead us
to amazing and
beautiful experiences.
Let go of the fear.

Sometimes it just takes a little lotion to clear dry skin. Try not to make things bigger than they are.

Trust in
yourself and the
universe that you
have everything
you truly need.
Once that deep
belief is there, all
of your desires will
be taken care of.

Keep it simple and
live through love.

Stop! Be still. Take a deep breath. What are you grateful for in this very moment?

Let down
your guard,
change course if
necessary, and
follow your true
passions as that is
your life purpose.

Your "flaws" are
very important.
They are part of the
human experience.
Recognize and learn
from them, which will
make the process of
changing them easier.

Sit outside,
close your eyes,
feel the air on
your body, and
listen to the sounds
of nature. Pay
attention to how
you feel. Then add
a few thoughts of
gratefulness.
Aahh.

When our "mind goes blank," it is trying to tell us we need a break. Take a few minutes to allow your mind to be still. Practice often.

Talking to
yourself is not
crazy. Talking down
to yourself is. Be your
own cheerleader!

We can learn much from the ancient ways. Think about how you can simplify your life to bring more joy.

Working through our head can be variable. Working through our heart is always spot on.

Spiritual
guidance is
everywhere. You
just need to open
your eyes, ears, and
heart to receive it.

Our bodies are talking to us emotionally and physically. Find out what it is saying and listen for a healthy and joyful life.

Fear causes
resistance. If
something does
not come easily, look
to see what fear is
connected to it.

Celebrate life!
Really think about
what that means.

Acting crazy can
be a release. Get
out there and
have some fun!

Things you
think you have
forgotten, your
soul remembers.
Nothing is ever
forgotten and you
can access them when
you truly want to. It is
all part of the journey.

Pursue your dreams. What are you waiting for? Start with the first step. Then you will know pure joy.

There is a
spiritual
connection
to everything.
Be quiet and still to
reflect on what it is
to bring peace.

Frustration,
like all emotions,
is a compass for
your well-being.
Acknowledge it,
understand it, let it go.

Good always comes from what we label "bad" situations. New opportunities, inner growth, new friendships, new views... There is always something. Be open to recognize them.

Love yourself
by saying
"I love you"
in the mirror
each morning.
Watch the positive
changes unfold.

Seeing
something
from a different
view can help
broaden your
perspective and
open the door to
send love where you
might not have before.

Letting go of
the past maybe
very difficult, but
it is extremely
important for your
physical and spiritual
well-being.
Forgiveness saves
YOU.

Sometimes annoyances are blessings. Look past the annoyances.

Treat each other
as if we were all
connected and
intertwined as one
because we are.

We often
make things
more difficult
than they need to
be. Do things from
the heart and
simplify your life.

Hovering over
a mountainside
or standing on
it will give you
different views of
the same terrain.
It is just a different
perspective.

Many things
that startle or
shake us now, we
laugh about later.
Find the humor
in it now.

Sometimes we can naturally avoid negativity, but sometimes we have to duck. Take action to bring positivity into your life.

Always be
conscious
of what you are
putting into your
body. Taking time
to enjoy it is just
as important.

Water is
cleansing.
Pay attention
in the moment
when bathing. Allow
your body to release
anything unwanted.
Then fill your body
with beautiful
white light.

When outside,
take notice
of your natural
surroundings. This
will not only bring
you to the present
moment, but will also
create calmness.

Just because
something does
not fit perfectly,
does not mean it is
useless. Some things
just need adjusting.

Things may
not go as you
planned, but they
are going as
planned. Trust
that everything is
as it should be and
you are loved.

If you want
kindness around
you, fill the space
with love.

Our instincts
naturally guide us
to pursue what is
best for us.

Paying attention
to our emotions
helps guide us. If
we feel off track
then we can stop,
breathe, and focus
on getting back on.

Belief is the
foundation of
existence. Believe
what you want can
be and it will.

Our inner light
only shines as
much as we allow
it. Be conscious
of what you are
sending out.

If you think of
something as an
inconvenience,
then it will be.

All you can be
is yourself. Just
be conscious
of who that is.

Rituals and habits bring us comfort. Make them good ones.

First thing in the morning is a good time to tell yourself how your day will be. Continue confirming it throughout the day and pay attention to how your day goes. What kind of day are you affirming?

Even during
stressful situations,
have fun.

When someone
comes to you with
angry words, they
are their words.
You do not own them.

Just as there is enough sun for all the oranges in the orchard, there is enough love for all the people in the world.

The more you
are open to the
universal energy
of love, the more
ease you will have
in your life and
less dis-ease.

Do not negate
your fantasies.
Your imagination
can manifest
amazing things.

We do not fail.
We experience.

Comparing
ourselves to others
only breeds jealousy
or superiority. We
are all human beings
experiencing life for
a purpose.

Young is in the
heart and the body
will follow.

Sit quietly and imagine your aura full of love. Repeat often.

Outer sight and
inner sight are
equally important.
They lead to insight.

There are two perspectives, one above the water and one below. We need to see both to see the full picture.

Stressing about
time only wastes
time. Affirm that
you have plenty of
time and focus on
the present moment.
Watch how your
perception of
time changes.

If something
does not feel right,
trust it. Your inner
knowing is the
best guide you
will ever have.

Think of life as
floating in a canoe
down a river. There
maybe turbulence
in spots, but there is
always calm again on
the other end.

Everyone makes
their own choices.
Allow them to live
with theirs while
you live with yours.

Trust in yourself
may be difficult,
but it is the most
important.

If your intuition
senses danger,
listen. Then use
your head to decide
what to do, not
dismiss it.

The breath is
the foundation
for the body, mind,
and spirit. Use it
consciously for
everything.

Beliefs are
extremely powerful.
Do yours promote
love and harmony
within yourself?

Growth is a process. Taking little steps at first can lead to great things.

It is okay to hold
onto traditions,
but it is also okay
to make new ones.

To get to where we
are going, we need
to take the steps.

Face your fears
and you may end
up having an
amazing experience.

Be happy where
you are rather
than looking to
the future and
more of what makes
you happy will be
where you are.

Be open to other's
ideas. It could
change your life.

Allow others to
be who they are as
you would expect
to be yourself.

Shine your light
to draw in people
who will appreciate it.

Believe in yourself
to manifest a joyous
and purposeful life.

The best gift you
can give yourself
is believing and
trusting you.

Stress causes physical ailments in the body. Take a deep breath and focus on something positive in the situation, no matter how small.

Promoting peace
within ourselves
helps promote peace
in our surroundings.

All that is needed
will come in time.

Doing things
through love will
get different results
than doing them
through fear.

Share your talents
with others to
bring joy to
yourself and them.

If you do not
like being
aggravated,
then do not be.
It is our choice
how we react.

There is no bad time. Everything is in divine order.

How will your
day go today?
Decide now.

There is energy in everything. Pay attention to your environment and how it makes you feel.

If you keep
going back to
something you love,
then incorporate
it somehow into
your every day.

When it comes to questions about your life, you know all the answers. You just need to remember them.

In all the world
there is no one like
you and you are
perfect.

Why do we feel
old, tired, sick?
Because we tell
ourselves we are.

Fear is the only
limitation we have.

35260567R00209

Made in the USA
Middletown, DE
26 September 2016